Saved to Cloud
Kate Foley

ARACHNE PRESS

First published in UK 2023 by Arachne Press Limited
100 Grierson Road, London, SE23 1NX
www.arachnepress.com
© Kate Foley 2023

ISBNs
Print: 978-1-913665-76-0

eBook: 978-1-913665-77-7

Printed on woodfree paper by TJ Books, Padstow, England.

Thanks to Muireann Grealy for her proofreading.

The publication of this book is supported using public funding by the National Lottery through Arts Council England.

Acknowledgements

Thanks to the following for original publication of some of these poems

12 Rivers, magazine of the Suffolk Poetry Society and their *The Ripples,* anthology celebrating the society's 70th birthday

Poetry Wivenhoe, anthology and poster exhibition

Artemis magazine of the Second Light group of women poets

The Friend, Quaker magazine

Words from the Brink, Solstice Shorts Festival 2021, Arachne Press

Saved to Cloud

for Tonnie

Contents

NECESSARY POETS

The ones you did for 'O' level,
live in your pocket
like a silver coin.
You rub an embossed head
with your thumb
to find a sovereign truth.
Ordinary poets
may from time to time,
if they're lucky
speak the one word
that will do, so
they need to learn humble –
because, if the arrow hits the target,
they'll never know.

THIS

This is my smartphone
            my app –
– a river of small birds
flows across the sky,
ripples in floodwater.

I try to write their words
in another language.
This

my life
my time
harvested
in ink.

This

is my computer,
shedding messages
like pigeon feathers
after the hawk.
Yes, I will mail you.
Promise!

This

is the new this,
Facetime they call it,
when the shining leaf
and the virus
both live outside

while we hope on
behind our windows and screens,
when gadgets and gizmos
offer a grateful substitute
for the touch
we long for.

POWER CUT

I'm sitting in candlelight,
black writing wavering on the page.

Yes! paper, pen and ink!
Making this tiny gesture,
two fingers up to keyboards,
screens, the febrile glow
of phones in faces, in trains,
on planes, at dinner,
under the pillow –
down the aisle...?

The algorithm
of my own life, faded
and spidery,
is written,
not keyed in.

No need to be complacent –
I still can't read it
and maybe never will,
but, thank you, candle,
meaning leaps in that flame
I can't read either.

Maybe the writing is enough.

BOOKS

Slivers of gold
as a flighty winter sun
eclipses bindings.

Books,
seen through a half-open door
while I drink my morning coffee.
Hidden contents
shimmy undetected,
as a sudden rainbow,
caused by a passing cloud
subverts the colour
of their jackets.

Never mind print.
Never mind magisterial
meaning. Who
needs to read
when light-show days
seduce with gold, or shadow,
and books
transcend all meaning
by simply being –
all the mystery of their light and dark,
alive on shelves?

THE EDUCATION OF THE HEART
(title of a book by Thomas Merton)

began long before
I hung on the front gate,
watching the other kids
kick the gravel
and lean backwards
against the wagging
finger of the day.

'WHY can't I go too, Mum?'
'When you're five,' she says

before
starched scholarship's
blue and gold,
before cockney lips
learned to roll out,
soft as chocolate
first words of French,
before can't-do,
won't-do
sums...

or was it perhaps
when lips first met lips,
or when the first thunk
of loss fell on a coffin?

Do ants, caterpillars, birds,
elephants, trees have educated hearts?

How do you 'educate'
that fat, turbulent, bloody muscle?

Can we take lessons?

NAN

Her thin grey hair
spitting hairpins,
her chin alive
with whiskers,
her black hem
draggled towards
her bunions.

'Ye beggars, ye!'
she'd shout,
glee thinly disguised.
She'd watched
and waited till we came.

One room,
a massive bed,
a tiny grate,
coal piled in the corner
under an oilskin shroud.

She never called me
by my christian name,
always kat'leenfoley,
making sure I knew
my borrowed status –
but a grudging ta
when Father O'Riley –

'Ogodogod – for Mrs Foley you say?'–
let me fill her whiskey bottle
with holy water from the font.

I only had one Nan.
The one I never had.
The one who, like a meteor
blundering over the skies
of childhood, taught me
how to remember.

ROSEBAY WILLOWHERB

climbed nimbly over
the broken bricks
of bomb-sites,
our playgrounds.

Those jagged slivers
of sinks, a lavatory
toppling out
of a leaning wall –

just right for playing
Mothers & Fathers; perfect
for Feet off the ground.
DON'T said my Mum.

'Aaaaw Mum!'
But we went anyway,
not equating the lit
night sky

or those lonely remnants
leaning out of the shattered brick
with death.

PLAIN

I wish my life
had been plain.

Not Habitat or Ikea
or designer kitchen plain

but like an ordinary table
meant for simple dishes,

holding up what is necessary.

Or even plain like the woodpecker,
his blazing red head

biffing the sparrows
at the birdfeeder,

since plain is not without
colour or complication

but is without pretension.

Although like water,
that plainest of stuff,

the best kind of love may be plain,
still it can follow

its own deepest underground
tracery of contradictions.

EGG

Yolk dribbles down
the freckled shell –
just the way
he likes it.

DUNK! Brown, buttery
toast dives in.
His fingers
can do that, still.

'Tssssk...' His carer
wipes the crumb encrusted
gloop from his chin.
'What about some music?'

she tells, not asks.
On goes the high
resolution memory
machine. Once,

hands were supple as willow
stems, fingers sang
in grasshopper leaps,
or languorous as a cat

stretched. Now music – his –
floods out. 'Who brought
that bloody cat in?'
he growls.

SLOWLY ACQUIRING SILVER

Worn the tee-shirt,
logos fading now –

Stop the...
Save the...
RESIST!

Now the sharpest sherds
of memory wear a soft bloom,
as a tiny beetle footprint
creates an unexpected
line of music
in the dust.

God has dropped off
like an old shoe.
Who cares? The laughter-
lines of water still crinkle
in my half-full glass

as I learn
grey is that nuance
where black is married
to white and silver
celebrates their wedding.

IN CAFE WELLING AMSTERDAM

in lockdown when we were all entertained by the tableau

'They shouldn't be there!' the woman snaps,
craning against the window to see.
Then 'Oh! OH!' and when she turns

we see a tear creep
into her mask. Inside,
wood panels glow

darkly. Beer pumps glisten,
behind the bar bottles wink,
the barmaid waits – smiling?

Punters sit, cradling half-full glasses.
A woman curls her lip, her man
is hang-dog. What's the story?

A couple lean together. Plastic and stuffing?
No! They pulse with should-shouldn't, will-
won't choices and moments.

A man, hunched against intrusion
reads the paper. This is memory,
paused but waiting for us.

The Cafe Welling is lit for us
with the warm shadowy
light of kindness.

TO LEARN A LANGUAGE

never mind prepositions
or irregular verbs –

there is nothing academic
about a peach,

a cat, a skyscraper, a bridge
over the dark water

you may come to love
but never understand the direction

of its flow.
Think you're not smart enough?

How do you
remember the contours of your lover's

body?
With fingertips, nose, eyes, ears.

That's how you
learn a language –

with love

A WALK IN THE PARK

where wild creeps into the laundered grass.

Like wrinkles on an old face,
tracks scurry to the dark holes
burrowed between tree roots,
and the green crowns of trees
sway and sing grand-opera,
each green so different
from its siblings
they might be basso-profundo,
resonant alto
or little-boy soprano,
all warbling in a harmony
of wind.

White as a tiny orange pip
a baby stork's head
peers over
the careful lacing
of its nest.

We walk,
as broken bark-chips shuffle
quietly under our feet.
Re-cycled in death
they speak
of trees.

ALL CHANGE

Walking among
the bric-a-brac
of days

      -doesn't the Co-op
       keep mustard anymore?
      -make sure those eggs
      are free-range
      -watching the local
      lambs frolic
      not yet upside down for the knife
      -how much in the Ukraine pot?
      a fiver?

–squeezing the odd tear
      out for the telly–
you wonder

if for one piercing moment
we could feel what they feel,
would anything change?

POLITICS

is that tall, dark, shiny
plate-glass window,
said to be transparent,
that reflects only what
those who want to see,
see.

One can tweak one's waistcoat
there, straighten one's tie,
insist that the government
has a plan – that greenhouse
gases will be reduced...
'In time?' you ask,

as the last bee in your garden
lumbers, painfully laden
to the last-but-one buttercup
and the butterfly, with one
fractured wing, limps across the air,
and the warbler who can't,

falls silent.

'THERE IS NO PLANET B'

says the caption on the man
stuck to the lamp-post,
with his chimney-pot head
belching out smoke,

but now as the sun-slipped summer
blazes in autumn street flowers,
a rampage of colour, flickering
with bees says, 'eh? –
who needs one?'

As we sit, drinking coffee,
in the heat-drenched park,
we never notice
how tree-speak,
the quiet language of roots,
curls deep underground,
hoarded, hidden,
in case the future
never happens.

Wiser than us,
perhaps the trees
have a point.

LINES

Old trees wear
the habit of spread.
Old women, too.

Tree crinkled wrinkles
host hummus, pools,
fertile dirt

in trunks and branches,
time-warped, still busy
with hospitality.

Old women also wear
their pilgrim paths
and some their laughter lines,

a web that spells
a life in hieroglyphs
only a mirror can read.

When the last old woman
has left the planet
how will the trees learn to laugh?

APOCALYPSE

'Thanks to our viewer who sent
this wonderful sunset photo.'
The weatherman doesn't say
'taken at six am today'.

Whitehall says
'no panic' so
got up this morning,
scratched our armpits,
climbed in the shower,
kissed the kids,
time to go.

Used as we are
to 'climate change'
they call it,
and now the piercing frost
of stars at night
is hidden in the glare
of our inferior suns,

we never see the outraged universe,
just but never kind,
thundering down the galaxies
to wipe us from its mind.

WAKE UP!

The small green cities
of trees
are running out of traffic.
Little lives of insects fall, hiss
their last in the wilting grass.
Birds limp onto branches
before their wings like rusted
hinges refuse
to fly.
The six o'clock news tells,
without telling,
what the weather is, but never
what it isn't.

Is the god we sing on Sunday
a poet run out of rhyme,
a song without music,
a lever that snapped
and lies on the landfill
of our once and future past?

Never mind god.
Tenderly part the plastic
from the aluminium foil.
Do the daft and useless
usefulnesses, clock-up
the smallest, busy points,
our substitute for prayer
and learn to mourn –

not from politicians,
the undertakers of earth,
but from our own
grieving
living
hearts,
the foetal
heart
of mercy.

REFRACTION

If I were to paint it
you'd never know
where to find it,
that source
of the blaze
on Cezanne's apples.
that wisp on the neck
of Vuilliard's sewing woman,
the deep shine of faith
in the face
of Old Woman Reading,
or the wink, lurking in the folds
of Rembrandt's bulbous nose.

If you look
you can find it in music,
on the bald head of a baby,
in the curve of hands touching
and even in the shadow
they make on the road.

When the last pheasant
is shot
and the sludge settles in the massive oil tanks
waiting for nobody,
when the last tree falls from the memory
of no one,
it will still be there,
skittering, pottering,
refracting.

TAKING THE KNEE
George Floyd murdered by police: May 2020

I can't be black.
I can't be poor.
I can't be foreign.

A knee on the neck.
Eviction.
A ruptured dinghy.

Every blown leaf
of a lost life
whispers

the truth of those
who lost it.
No comfort

for our shuttered
ears and eyes –
or them –

in the tree-ring
growth
of sorrow.

OUR (OLD) LADY
April 15 2019: fire at Notre Dame

Centuries: an eyelid flutter.
Millennia: a Saurian wink.
Aeons: and
stone evolves,
fire in its veins,
cools.

The workmen's blunt, prehensile
hands held fire-forged sharpness
to cut meaning, messages,
jokes, ribaldry, faces, growing
out of the banked fires
of stone, as they balanced
on the swaying ghosts of forest trees.

If they fell
their widows would shuffle
down the long aisles
to the altar
and a wafer-thin
consolation.

Now their descendants swarm
on singing metal frames,
smoothing cracks,
blisters, wrinkles.

She needs to be mended.

Like an old shoe,
she has cradled the feet
of our journey.

We are not ready to be motherless.

TEA TIME

Now that I know
that prayer's impossible
the question is
not how to live
but how to keep on dying.

I'm no leaf
to blaze until
abscission's final click.
There has to be some slight, uneasy grace,
one that deserves the name
of grace, unwilled
and undeserved,
an accidental light.

Like a sudden stone,
a feather,
an empty shoe,
it speaks
of sweat and feet
and marries then with now.

Nothing up-market.
No Buddha, Christ
no tree of mystery
of leaves or nails

but simple as a cup of tea,
when gas ignites
and water boils
and thirst still waits
but comfort's
in the curve of hands accepting.

WHAT I KNEW ONCE

How I knew then,
sorting stones in the back alley,
that they came from fire
and the thunder
of earth shaking off
magma and flame,

how I knew
that the spider on the back
gate drew a marvellous
map with silk,
a living harp
to sing winged creatures in,

how I knew then
that foetal seed in the rough
pit of plums
would flicker like a time-lapsed
photo into blossom, stamen, pollen,
fruit with bloom

purple as a bruise
or cloud, I don't know.
Cousin to the hens,
dandelions, chickweed,
small niece of weather,
I only knew
  I knew
what I've long forgotten.

Only the ouch of nettles,
soothe of dock, scuffle of newborn chicks,
garden dust on our round-toed shoes,
hot electric fur of a neighbour's cat
burn memory back to one-ness
with a child in a world she knew.

THE DYING ZONE

When they ask
'do you want to be resuscitated?'
and '...it depends'
is not a good enough answer,

when dreams
become a shred of chiffon,
a mere
fog on your spectacles,

not the full bellied
prayer flags
straining on the winds of hope
you thought,

will you put up
with the long waiting-room
ennui, as those
before you in the queue

disappear and the shuffle
of newspapers releases
the scent of old print?
Or will you finally

discover the scripture
of the sane is absence,
and trace with the braille
alphabet of your fingers

the raised letters
that still, for the brave
enough, spell love?

IN THE CAVE OF NIAUX

At first we are tourists
but we morph into visitors,
treading the thin glaze of damp underfoot,
gingerly, as if it were
their hall carpet.

We hear messages,
a drum?
a thin bone pipe?
a vibrating gut
from an animal that time forgot?

Wild vowels swoop
round the echoes,
guttural consonants
hiss and scratch
like a scatter of flint.

The breath that sprays ochre
round their widespread
signature hands

sings

to the herds that flock
on the dark face
of the rock.

How the past fingerprints the present,
so every trace, smudge and contour
is art.

TREE-SPEAK

Then, before it all changed,
the ancient tree-line curved
around the flank of the spare,
bare, silent hill above.

Now there are no humans
but trees keep their long recollections
as knots in the rough
furrows of their bark,
with a tiny pin-point of history
packed into every seed
sent spinning
on the wind
that is their only memory of wings,
their messenger
and lover,
throwing great wanton
clouds of pollen,
up, up.

Now that leaves
are the dominant language,
forgotten words lie
like broken bricks,
love and despair
transmuted
into the rosebay willowherb.

A MURMURATION

They drift, scatter,
darken the sky,
wheel, suddenly curl,
spiral, become a fragile
loop of smoke
in the sunset
like tea-leaves emptied out
from a great spout
hidden behind a cloud

Too far away, too high
to hear we fill
that distance
with the imagined
hushhhh of wings,
not knowing that those sharp-edged
bony implements of flight
sound like a battalion
of angry women opening
their fans,
or that the voice
of their swirling, elegant churn
shrieks like the ancient brakes
of a vintage train.

We know what we have seen.

Leave us our dream.

ON BEING 80 PLUS

My days are a Stately Progression,
stitched into a corset less malleable
than whalebone. My skirts do not whisper.
They creak like a rusty key.
Skirts? Me? I'm a dyke! Don't wear 'em.
'Now' says that strict, not-to-be-gainsayed
Governess, Time, 'you will wear
what you have become. Middling.
Not-very. More-or-less-ish.'
She doesn't mean middle-aged, either.
'Not even one ride on a broomstick?'
I ask. 'If you can find one,' she says,
more kindly. 'Look for the moon.
It's easier to find than the sun.'

WHAT FOR

'What's it all for?'
my father asked grumpily
before he died.

Was it for his tools,
oiled, sharp,
their handles polished

by his big careful hands?
Or the garden,
where well-tended hens

scratched, and Blondie,
my rabbit, sat
till we ate her?

Was it for my Mum,
who lumbered out of bed
and sat in that chair

her neighbour wanted
and died? One last
One Up, Mum!

Was it for his queer
unsatisfying daughter,
adopted when you didn't

but he did, they did,
and she received
as a gift

one last long look
from his fading eyes.

TOOLBOX

Now that I have that swing,
heft of the belt,
settling of the hips

in my words,
I can say what my body
never could.

Scrim, coulter, onomatopoeia,
adamant – thin words,
fat words, words barely understood,

some jumbled together in a rusty
bucket, some laid out,
in my toolbox

with that sharp, flayed grin
of readiness to cut deep.
Sometimes I swagger a little –

but sometimes I remember
the big blunt hands of my father
as he blessed his tools

to sleep on their shelves
in the simple cupboard
of his timid heart.

BEACHCOMBING

I'm picking up words,
stones from the beach,
some felted with sand,
some hiding a fossil past,
some dull, lustreless
but weighty.

Their heft in my hand,
their shape,
their hop-skip-jump
as they skim,
tells me what
I must say.

I want my words
worked like arrowheads,
flints picked up and spread
on distant fields,
timeless,
still cutting-edge sharp.

When the fire in the heart
of this rocky ball dies
what will the last
word
left alive
say?

COLLECTIONS

An Iron Age burial: woman, child, foetal pig.
Museum drawers full of Birds of Paradise,
flattened like faded gloves.

Iron Age? Time-lapsed. You can see
from the glassy edges of the bones
how loss and life blood rubbed away

and the Paradise birds, their strut and preen studied,
their live wings
at least recorded while still warm.

But all the helpless shoes piled up for the cameras.
We see them only on tv.
Not yet archaeology.

So far no-one's research collection,
so you can't hear the terrible hush
of their emptying.

MY FAVOURITE POEM?

Hmm... how can you have
a favourite? They shift
every day like clouds,
sometimes awe-inspiring,
giants, sometimes playful,
sometimes weeping with failure,
with only one line piercing
like a spear of rain.
A cloud perhaps
is the closest thing to a poem.
It holds weather to its heart
and we don't know
whether the rain will fall,
the wind creep up from nowhere
or the sun slip through –
and as for sunlight,
falling, interspersed with
shadows
as I write,
is that a better image
for the fitfulness of poems?
But cloud, sun, midnight,
noon, my favourite
is always the one
that speaks, direct
plain-faced and earthed,
to the hidden places
of my heart today.

DEAR POEM

isn't it rather chilly
to be regarded as an exchange of energy?
Or a packet of potential? Wouldn't you rather be
actual?
If you're going to lurk out there, hovering
like the creak of a door in the wind,
at least come a little closer.

This is risky of course. You might
be a handwringer, establishing your status
on the outskirts of my life. O god! You might
be macho and stride through the corridor
of our dream, easing
your blokeish trousers.

You might be old without wisdom.
No. I see you, clear, contained,
silvery, with a capable heart
made of some precious metal
which may catch fire. Fluid as a minnow,
your shape changes as fast as you move.

Let's get intimate. Move me.
You can borrow my blood and bones
if you let me feel the burnt silver slap
of your absent hand on the skin of my heart
and wake me.

Shall we risk it?

SLOW WATER

the Water Detectives
call it

searching as it runs below
the veins and arteries
of the land,

buried
in the history of rocks,
the strata of soil,

quiet influencer
of all that grows –

as poetry,
winding below
the culverts

of every day,
sometimes hidden,
sometimes bursting

over the map
of being
is surely

the slow water
of our souls.

JUST A LINE

'Writing is drawing'
she said.

'Oh yeah?!
My line is
      w
        o
          b
            b
              l
                  y.......'

Pavements, faces, skyscrapers,
kite tails, vapour trails,
a lifeline in your palm,
the line that keeps
your life in.

Do you cross it
in sleep?
How? When?

Draw one
every day.
Never mind the full stop.

YOU THINK YOU HEAR THEM SING

Little clouds climb on the wind,
commute, flocking over the flatland fields.
Birds or clouds?
Your ears stretch to catch a snatch of song.

Does the fox, curved
round the distant wood-edge
hear? Are the rooks squawking
in a ploughed field answering?
Are the moles, piling their brown
cakes of soil deaf as well
as blind?

So many sounds we'll never hear,
the crunch of charcoal on a cave wall,
that splattering brush that laid
those images down,
the creak of a pen on parchment,

but with the ears of our hearts
we know we hear their song.

SUNDAY MORNING

Belief. Too heavy a word
to cross that eye-widening
leap of the heart
at buds still budding
almost as if
nothing's happening.

That little globe,
our human world,
like a paperweight
when you make it snow,
floats above the simpler world
of birds, leaves – and viruses.

Somewhere men with shovels
are burying the dead,
while those whose smoke
is given to air, alive with birds,
find their own memorial
in clouds.

Is it too much to hope, perhaps,
we'll lose that weighty doorstop,
belief, and find instead
our faith, our place, our joy and loss,
as creatures in the world
of birds, leaves and viruses?

A NEW LANGUAGE

Her eyes widen
above her mask.
Is she smiling?

or have I
come too close?
I smile

and hope our wordless
interaction means
what we both intend.

We sidle past
each other in shops,
in streets

where shops are closed.
We smile at little dogs
and kids

and hope our speaking
fingers
tell our meanings

and from the canal side's
naked winter-stripped
old trees

we learn
that messages
are more than words.

GOD IS THE POEM

I go to meet
but never do,
in special places
where god is written
in pictogram,
in hieroglyph,
in cursive,
in best italic script,
on the foreheads
of those
who rendezvous.

Eyes have lids
but earlids,
though unknown
in nature,
baffle the voice
I know that others hear.

No plangency
intended.
Instead, I mark
the scrawl of grass,
fighting to grow,
the heave and suck
of muck,
of insects in a soil,
made of countless
creatures, leaves,
the impress of dead feet,
a feather
and a scrap of rabbit poo.

I light
a candle to the virgin,
to the woodwose,
and all our myths.
That will do.

RAGS AND BONES

'Ra-bo-ooon'
   the old man sang.
Hooves of his pony,
creak of his cart,
shift and swing of his cargo
beat
 ta-ta-ta
   to his song.

He's gone –
so much rubbish,
smoke,
landfill spilling
on a once green land.

Choked mudflats ooze,
whisper, crackle,
heave the shoreline
into bundles –
Lego soldiers,
rusted bottle tops,
pet food cans,
stain of the rag
washed by stain of the river

and fractured bones,
their tender once-upon-a-time white
now chestnut rich –
an irony of rust.

ON FIRST SEEING www.quakeranimals.org

While earth, great dumb stepchild of the sun
lumbers slowly round First Day again,
a dusty caravan clops and pads
up the steps to the meeting house.

Each creature carries a weight of silence far
deeper than words can find, each knows in every hair
and hoof and paw, feather or fur, unspoken watchfulness
but comes, just for an hour to lay it there.

A donkey stretches his ancient back but keeps his cross,
two elderly cats, a rabbit and a rat knit their paws,
the cow rests her heavy luggage on a convenient bench
and rumbles quietly. A hiss of sheathing, of retracted claws.

Only a monkey, eldered twice, mutters, sulks
upside down from the lamp's bald electric wire.
Tigers, unlikely to subscribe to Peace, are held in light
but not invited, except to the safe perimeter of prayer.

Dear Quaker Animals, how like your two-legged
Friends you wait,
gentle for this morning, mild of face,
if slightly worn and puzzled,
deep in the thickets round the watering hole of grace.

LIMPING

Folded wrinkles ironed-in
to their lopped trunks.
Green olive leaves, barbered.
Gravel raked. Waiters
sewn into their white shirts.

But the sun flickers
in the boundary hedge
and we see a pigeon
make strange dance-steps.

First he hirples to a couple,
picking at their starter platter,
wine at their sides. No luck.
They know feeding's not kind...

Closer. We see one high
shoulder, a twisted neck –
and can it be? – a missing wing.
Bright eyes ask, not beg.

Not good for him, the salt…
but melted, we throw a peanut.
He flings himself at it –
another as he grinds
over the gravel –
snap, swallow, ask…

When we leave
he launches his ungainly body,
crooked as a falling leaf
and for a moment
floats.

A DAY WITHOUT A HERON

portly, grey,
staring into a dark mirror,
is a day without
water or sky

    but
a seagull, knot
of blood, bone, feathers
spread on a pounce
of wind
echoes the weather
you missed.

How can a leaf
dancing in the wake of a gull
write
the soul's weather
so we learn
to read?

VISITING THE BAYEUX TAPESTRY

If, as I suspect, you are a metaphor,
god,
how did it all happen –

the birds, raining past my window,
the sheep, bales of wool, sleeping
in the field,
the buds, some fighting to get born,
some hesitating on the trees.

It's all happening again,
just like the clot of severed crimson
threads, marking their fallen lives –

swords or missiles,
what's the difference, god?

We who can't enter
the small heads of birds
to understand their flight
want to know

REPEATING PATTERNS

Will it build again,
our earth?
Will it be nest
with rambling, seeded
stems and breast curved
feathers –
or den?
Will the first new atom
know who to marry?
Will creatures
glide, elide
through air or water?
Will they click and pick
on legs or fins or flick
their way on wings?
Will there be eyes and ears
and tongues when memories
lie millennia below
the fears we'd long forgotten
before we let them happen?